THE BERMUDA TRIANGLE

BY SUE HAMILTON

VISIT US AT
WWW.ABDOPUBLISHING.COM

Published by ABDO Publishing Company, 8000 West 78th Street, Suite 310, Edina, Minnesota 55439.
Copyright ©2008 by Abdo Consulting Group, Inc. International copyrights reserved in all countries.
No part of this book may be reproduced in any form without written permission from the publisher.
ABDO & Daughters™ is a trademark and logo of ABDO Publishing Company.

Printed in the United States.

Editor: John Hamilton
Graphic Design: Sue Hamilton
Cover Design: Neil Klinepier
Cover Illustration: Waterspout, Corbis
Interior Photos and Illustrations: p 4 Map, Cartesia/Hamilton; p 5 June 1930 *Amazing Stories*, Mary
Evans Picture Library; p 6 Christopher Columbus portrait, Sebastiano del Piombo; p 7 Columbus in
the Sargasso Sea, North Wind Picture Archives; Compass, iStockphoto; p 9 Avenger torpedo bombers,
Corbis; p 10 PBM Mariner Seaplane, U.S. Coast Guard; p 11 Ft. Lauderdale Naval Air Station, Getty;
p 12 Radar, Corbis; p 13 Map, Cartesia/Hamilton; p 14 Bahamas aerial view, Corbis; Florida Keys aerial
view, Corbis; p 15 Deep See Company, Getty; p 16 SS *Marine Sulphur Queen*, The Mariner's Museum;
Argosy magazine cover and article, *Argosy* magazine; p 17 Map, Cartesia/Hamilton; Captain J.V. Fanning,
AP Images; pp 18-19 SS *Marine Sulphur Queen* debris, U.S. Coast Guard; pp 20-21 SS *Marine Sulphur
Queen* debris, U.S. Coast Guard; p 22 Cabin cruiser, Corbis; p 23 Sailboat in rough seas, Getty; Buoy and
ship, U.S. Coast Guard; pp 24-25 Plane illustrations and photo of Bruce Gernon, courtesy Bruce Gernon;
p 26 Alien in flying saucer, iStockphoto; p 27 Plane flying into big cloud, Getty; p 28 Waterspout, Corbis;
p 29 Rogue wave, National Oceanic and Atmospheric Administration, p 31 Waterspout, Corbis

Library of Congress Cataloging-in-Publication Data

Hamilton, Sue L., 1959-
  The Bermuda Triangle / Sue Hamilton.
     p. cm. -- (Unsolved mysteries)
  Includes index.
  ISBN 978-1-59928-834-5
  1. Bermuda Triangle--Juvenile literature. I. Title.

G558.H36 2008
001.94--dc22

2007014553

CONTENTS

TRIANGLE OF MYSTERY

Bermuda is a series of beautiful islands lying east of the United States in the Atlantic Ocean. However, for all its sand, sun, and surf, it is one point of a mysterious area known as the Bermuda Triangle. Also called the Devil's Triangle, this area ranges from Bermuda to the island of Puerto Rico to Florida, and then back to Bermuda. Dozens of experienced ship captains and aircraft pilots have lost their lives in this alluring yet treacherous area.

Known as the graveyard of the Atlantic, this vast open triangle of water measures roughly 440,000 square miles (1,140,000 sq km). The weather is notoriously unpredictable. Brutal tropical storms can appear in a matter of minutes. For an inexperienced navigator, this can be a death sentence.

Since this area is one of the most heavily traveled places in the world, it is no surprise that many people have been tragically lost within the Bermuda Triangle. This is especially true of amateur pilots and sailors. But many professional sea captains and trained military pilots have also become victims. One moment they are in radio contact, and the next moment nothing is heard but static. Radar screens suddenly go blank.

More than 100 ships and 1,000 people have disappeared without a trace while traveling in the Bermuda Triangle. What happened to them? There are many ideas and theories, including alien abductions, hurricanes, and human errors. The disappearances have brought researchers, scientists, geologists, historians, and even the United States Coast Guard to look deeper into the unexplained mysteries of the Bermuda Triangle.

Below: A map showing the mysterious area known as the Bermuda Triangle. It runs from Bermuda to Puerto Rico to Florida and back to Bermuda.

Bermuda

Florida

The Bermuda Triangle

Atlantic Ocean

Caribbean Sea

Puerto Rico

Above: The June 1930 issue of *Amazing Stories* featured "The Non-Gravitational Vortex" by A. Hyatt Verrill, one of the first stories about the Bermuda Triangle.

COLUMBUS DISCOVERS THE BERMUDA TRIANGLE

Christopher Columbus, during his 1492 expedition to the New World, experienced strange happenings in the unexplored waters of the Bermuda Triangle. The great explorer's ships floated for several days in the steamy, nearly windless area known as the Sargasso Sea. Named after the blanketing patches of brown sargassum seaweed that cover the waters, the Sargasso Sea is an area of calm within the Bermuda Triangle. The strong currents and wild waters of the Atlantic Ocean swirl around it.

More than 500 years ago, Admiral Columbus documented several odd occurrences while traveling through the Sargasso Sea. On September 13, 1492, it was noted that the ships' compasses were off. "On this day at the beginning of night the compasses northwested and in the morning they northeasted somewhat." Ten days later Columbus noted that "…the sea rose high and without wind…."

The crew fearfully wondered what odd place they had sailed into. Would they get out alive? Even Columbus reportedly wrote in his journal, "There exists the possibility of never leaving this legendary sea." Mutiny was in the air, but Columbus convinced the sailors that there had to be a logical explanation for these weird events.

A compass points northward unless there's an outside magnetic force nearby, such as magnetite, a mineral found in iron ore.

Below: A portrait of Christopher Columbus by the famous Italian artist Sebastiano del Piombo.

It's possible that a ship's carpenter accidentally placed a bucket of iron nails too close to the compass, which caused it to behave erratically. But perhaps there was an even more likely explanation.

A compass does not point to true north, Earth's exact northerly center point at the North Pole. Instead, a compass finds magnetic north, a point close to, but not exactly on, the North Pole. To make matters even more complicated, compass readings can vary by several degrees at different locations on the planet. Today's navigators know about this fact and can adjust for it. In 1492, Columbus knew that compasses could give false readings when ships sailed toward China. He guessed the same thing might occur when sailing westward. Columbus, perhaps without knowing why, may have figured out the riddle of his misbehaving compass.

But what of the sea rising? What force could move the sea without wind? Some researchers suggest that Columbus' ships were actually on the edge of the Sargasso Sea. Perhaps they had reached one of the strong currents that surround the area. Another explanation is that they witnessed the effects of a small undersea earthquake.

Finally, on October 11, Columbus spotted a light "like a wax candle rising and falling" in the distance. Odd lights have been seen by many people in the Bermuda Triangle. For Columbus, who found land the next day, the lights remained a mystery. Perhaps they came from a native village, or a distant fisherman in his boat. More than 500 years later, the answer still eludes us.

Above: Columbus' 1492 expedition was stuck for several days in the Sargasso Sea. The explorer would be the first to report unusual happenings in the area that became known as the Bermuda Triangle.

Below: An antique navigational compass.

FLIGHT 19: THE LOST PATROL

In 1945, 6 planes and 27 men vanished inside the Bermuda Triangle. This incident became known as the mystery of Flight 19. No trace of the men or their planes was ever found. The tragedy of Flight 19 sparked much interest in the odd happenings within the Bermuda Triangle. Over the years, facts and details of the case became blurred, combining myth with reality. What is the truth to Flight 19's unexplained disappearance?

The popular story of U.S. Navy Flight 19 begins on December 5, 1945. At 2:00 P.M., five TBM Avenger torpedo bombers with 14 airmen aboard took off from the U.S. Naval Air Station in Fort Lauderdale, Florida. It was a day fliers live for: clear and sunny. Lieutenant Charles Taylor, an experienced pilot, was in command of Flight 19. It was supposed to be a simple two-hour training mission. Their orders were to fly due east for 150 miles (241 km), north for 40 miles (64 km), and then return to base. However, one hour and 45 minutes into the mission, something went wrong.

At 3:45 P.M. the Fort Lauderdale air-traffic control tower reportedly received a transmission from the flight leader: *"Cannot see land. We seem to be off course."* The tower asked for their position. The flight leader didn't know where they were, stating, *"We cannot be sure where we are. Repeat: Cannot see land."*

By 4:15 P.M., the tower still could not locate Flight 19. Another transmission came through, but not from the flight leader. This time someone else was on the radio. The frightened airman stated, *"We can't tell where we are... can't make out anything. We're completely lost."*

Minutes later, a PBM Mariner seaplane took off with a 13-member crew. Filled with rescue equipment, the seaplane headed toward what was believed to be the last known position of Flight 19.

Neither the five Avengers, the Mariner seaplane, nor any of the Navy personnel, were ever seen again.

Facing Page: Five Avenger torpedo bombers. Often called "Iron Birds," these were heavy, rugged planes built to withstand attacks.

Even after days of searching, no flare, oil slick, life raft, or piece of wreckage was ever found. The five Avenger bombers and the Mariner seaplane disappeared without a trace.

Above: A PBM Mariner seaplane similar to the one that took off looking for Flight 19. The Mariners were nicknamed "flying gas tanks." Designed for long scouting and rescue operations, the flying boats carried large amounts of fuel. Pilots sometimes worried that a spark would ignite an explosion.

What happened to the planes? Some claim they were taken by aliens. Others say a strange magnetic fog, found only within the Bermuda Triangle, caused serious compass and instrument failures. The United States Navy conducted an official investigation. The Navy's Board of Inquiry interviewed everyone involved, reviewed logs of the radio transmissions, and obtained opinions from experts, which shed light on the mystery. The actual facts vary quite a bit from the story as it's been told over the years.

Lt. Charles Taylor, the man in charge of the mission, was indeed an experienced combat pilot, having logged more than 2,500 hours of flying time. However, Taylor had just transferred to Fort Lauderdale from Miami, Florida. He had never flown this particular route. The other four pilots, and the nine enlisted crewmen, each had about 300 hours of flying time. They were just beginning their training in the Avengers. With only about 60 hours flying time in the torpedo bombers, they were still an inexperienced group.

The weather report for the area was listed as "favorable." However, that measurement was taken in the morning. Flight 19 went out shortly after 2:00 P.M. Another training flight, which had left an hour earlier, noted favorable weather, but also observed moderate to rough seas.

After takeoff, Lt. Taylor followed the other four planes in a tracking position. His plane's call sign was Fox Tare Two Eight (FT-28). Carefully checked out before departing, each of the Avengers was loaded with bombs for glide-bombing practice.

Each plane had a full gas tank. The planes could stay aloft for more than five hours, twice the time needed to complete the training mission.

Everything seemed to be going as expected until after the bombing training. At that point, the team apparently got turned around. A senior flight instructor happened to be flying over the Fort Lauderdale area at the time and overheard a confused radio exchange. A man named Powers, one of the trainees of Flight 19, reportedly stated, *"I don't know where we are. We must have got lost after that last turn."*

The flight instructor, whose call sign was FT-74, informed the Fort Lauderdale tower, and then sent a message, *"This is FT-74, plane or boat calling 'Powers' please identify yourself so someone can help you."*

Powers did not reply, but Lt. Taylor identified himself as FT-28. When asked his trouble, Taylor replied, *"Both my compasses are out and I am trying to find Fort Lauderdale, Florida. I am over land but it's broken. I am sure I'm in the Keys but I don't know how far down and I don't know how to get to Fort Lauderdale."*

Above: An overall view of the Fort Lauderdale Naval Air Station. Flight 19 took off from this location on December 5, 1945, never to return.

The flight instructor offered to help by flying to Taylor's position over the Florida Keys, the chain of islands off the state's southern coast. Taylor declined the help. *"I know where I am now,"* Taylor replied. *"Don't come after me."* But minutes later FT-28 was back on the air, *"Can you have Miami or someone turn on their radar gear and pick us up? We don't seem to be getting far. We were out on a navigation hop and on the second leg I thought they were going wrong, so I took over and was flying them back to the right position. But I'm sure, now, that neither one of my compasses is working."* Taylor was told to turn on his IFF gear, an emergency signal, which he reportedly did.

By 4:26 P.M., the Air-Sea Rescue Task Unit at Fort Everglades heard from FT-28, asking if anyone had a radar screen that could pick them up. The message was relayed all around the area, but there were problems. Several ships and towers never received the notice because of electronic equipment failure. And when an attempt was made to find Flight 19's position based on their radio transmissions, static and radio broadcasts from Cuba prevented the searchers from getting an accurate signal.

Below: A 1944 photo of military personnel watching a radar scope. Lt. Taylor, commander of Flight 19, asked for location help, but the five Avenger torpedo bombers were not found on local radar equipment.

Still, 20 different land facilities began searching for Flight 19. Ships in the area, both commercial and military, as well as the Coast Guard, were looking for the five Avengers. Where were they?

By 4:45 P.M., Flight 19 was still lost. Air-Sea Rescue Task Unit 4 radioed to FT-28, asking Taylor to broadcast on the search and rescue frequency, but Taylor refused. *"I cannot switch frequencies,"* he said. *"I must keep my planes intact."*

Minutes ticked by. Two different students were overheard saying, *"If we could just fly west we would get home; head west."*

Whatever transpired in the air is unknown. But by 5:16 P.M., Taylor called once again, trying to report his position and stating that they would fly *"until we hit the beach or run out of gas."*

A little after 6:00 P.M., Taylor was heard to say, *"We may as well just turn around and go east again."* Clearly, Taylor believed they were over the Gulf of Mexico. However, his students believed they were over the Atlantic Ocean. On the ground, using radio signals, searchers calculated the planes to be north of the Bahamas and east of Florida. Unfortunately, Flight 19 did not get that information. And the weather over the Bahamas had become a pilot's nightmare: poor visibility and darkening skies.

At 6:20 P.M., a final transmission was picked up from Taylor. *"All planes close up tight... we'll have to ditch unless landfall... when the first plane drops below 10 gallons, we all go down together."*

Reports were now coming in of high winds and rough seas in the area. Two PBM Mariners, U.S. Navy patrol bombers often used in air-sea rescue missions, were diverted from a training flight to join in the search. One of the planes, PBM-5, with three aviators and a crew of 10, lost contact and was never heard from again.

Did the crew of PBM-5 stumble into the same dire situation as Flight 19? Were the aircraft taken by an outside force? Did a strange fog wreck havoc with all the planes?

After its investigation, the Navy Board of Inquiry stated that the cause of Flight 19's disappearance was confusion on the part of Lt. Taylor. Taylor's mother did not believe her experienced son could have made such a mistake. The Navy later changed the wording of the Board of Inquiry report, stating that Flight 19 disappeared because of "causes or reasons unknown." However, many believe confusion was indeed the cause. Lt. Taylor may have mistaken the cays of the northern Bahamas for the islands that make up the Florida Keys.

Below: A faulty compass may have been responsible for Flight 19 being off course.

Taylor and the students of Flight 19 argued about their position. Apparently, no compasses were working, or Taylor believed they were malfunctioning.

It's possible that when the five planes' fuel ran low, they ditched into the ocean. This would have been a death sentence. Even the most experienced pilot would find it nearly impossible to land safely in a rough sea, with heavy winds, in the dark. Even if the planes miraculously made it down intact, the heavy 14,000-pound (6,350-kg) Avengers (known as "Iron Birds") would have sank quickly to the ocean depths.

The Bahamas

The Florida Keys

Right: A modern-day aerial view of the Bahamas and of the Florida Keys. Lt. Taylor may have confused the two locations, thinking he was in the Florida Keys, but was instead over the Bahamas. At the time, in 1945, many of the modern buildings and roads were not yet built. For someone unfamiliar with the area, it would have been easy to confuse the two locations.

But what of the PBM Mariner aircraft? The plane, nicknamed the "flying gas tank," was an explosion waiting to happen. Pilots often collected matches and cigarettes from airmen, knowing that the least spark could ignite any stray gas fumes in the plane. PBM-5 was loaded with hundreds of gallons of fuel, enough to stay airborne for 12 hours.

At around 7:50 P.M., the captain of the tanker ship *Gaines Mills* sent a message: *"...observed a burst of flames, apparently an explosion, leaping flames 100 feet high and burning for ten minutes."* The ship searched for survivors, but found none. Later, the USS *Solomons* reported that PBM-5 disappeared from their radar screen at that exact spot. Although people continue to question the disappearance, logic points to the fact that the plane may have had a gas leak. A small spark could have caused a massive explosion, leaving very little wreckage to be found in a vast ocean.

In 1991, a salvage ship discovered the wreckage of five Avengers off the coast of Florida. People were sure the "Lost Patrol" had finally been found. But the planes turned out to be part of a group of eight bombers that were lost during practice runs in the area. To this date, no wreckage has ever been found of Flight 19. Many argue about what really happened to Flight 19 and PBM-5. The facts point toward errors and accidents. Still, some people wonder about the mysterious forces of the Bermuda Triangle.

SS MARINE SULPHUR QUEEN

Above Right: The SS *Marine Sulphur Queen* in 1944.
Below Left & Right: The February 1964 *Argosy* magazine, in which author Vincent Gaddis first wrote about the Bermuda Triangle.

The first person who used the term "Bermuda Triangle" may have been author Vincent Gaddis. He wrote an article for *Argosy* magazine in February 1964. The article explored the mysterious case of the SS *Marine Sulphur Queen*, a fully loaded tanker vessel that disappeared in the Bermuda Triangle in February 1963.

What is unusual about the *Marine Sulphur Queen*'s disappearance is that items from the ship were actually found in the waters off Florida. But because no radio distress message was ever heard, and no bodies of the ship's 39 crewmen were ever found, people wonder what really happened to the ship and those aboard.

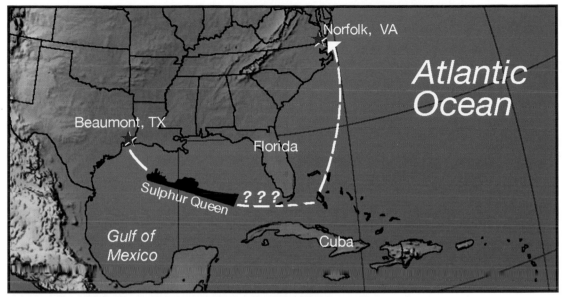

Above: A map of the *Marine Sulphur Queen*'s path, part of which led the ship through the Bermuda Triangle.

On February 2, 1963, the *Marine Sulphur Queen* left its port in Beaumont, Texas. Filled to capacity, the ship weighed 15,260 tons (13,844 metric tons). It was headed for the shipyards in Norfolk, Virginia, where its leaky cargo tanks were scheduled for repair. Several fires had broken out in the insulation between the ship's walls and the cargo tanks. But the small fires had always been quickly extinguished, and no one seemed worried about the *Marine Sulphur Queen*'s ability to make the trip.

Early on February 4, at 1:25 A.M., a crew member sent a personal message on the ship's radio transmitter, which apparently was working fine. It would be the last message ever heard from the ship. Later that day, two attempts were made to contact the *Marine Sulphur Queen*, neither of which got through. The ship was facing rough seas, with high winds and waves as tall as 16 feet (5 m). The message senders wondered if the weather was interfering with the radio's reception.

Below: Captain J.V. Fanning, skipper of the lost *Marine Sulphur Queen*.

Above: A life ring and a life jacket from the *Marine Sulphur Queen* are examined by U.S. Coast Guardsmen. A man's shirt is tied to the life ring.

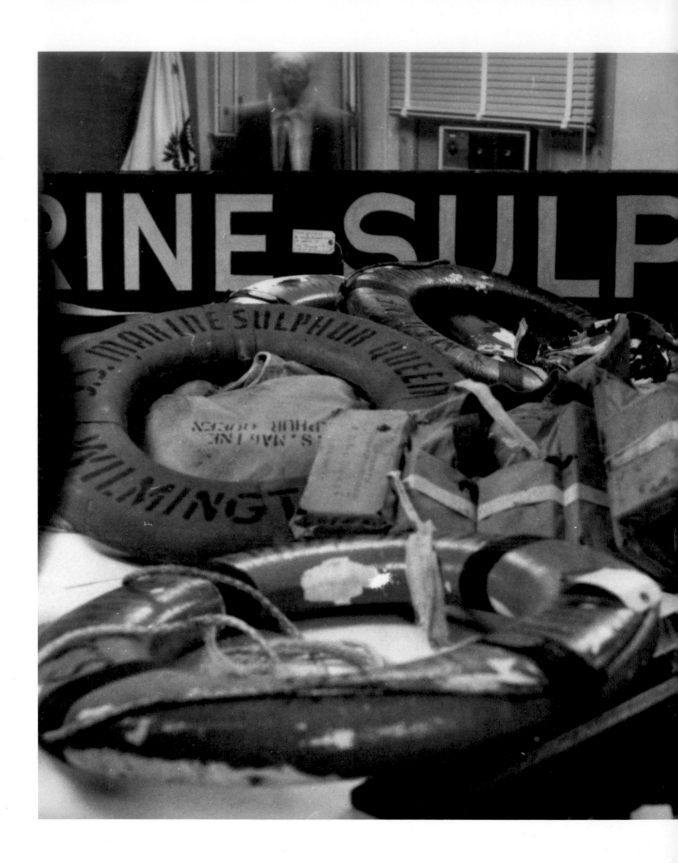

Three days later, at 9:00 P.M. on February 7, the *Marine Sulphur Queen* was reported overdue to the Coast Guard station in Portsmouth, Virginia. For the next five days, 83 air-sea rescue flights searched for the ship, covering 348,400 square miles (902,352 sq km).

Finally, on February 20, near Key West, Florida, a U.S. Navy vessel found a life preserver and foghorn with the *Marine Sulphur Queen*'s name on them. This brought renewed efforts to find the missing ship. Divers even searched underwater. Although more items were found, including eight life jackets and five life rings, one of which had a shirt tied to it, the 524-foot (160-m) ship and all aboard had vanished. On March 14, the search ended.

What happened to the *Marine Sulphur Queen*? Why was no radio SOS sent? Even if a huge explosion destroyed the ship's radio, the ship's lifeboat also had a portable radio. Had the Bermuda Triangle's mysterious forces kept the radios from working? And where were the survivors? Were they really dead? Or had some unknown being captured them?

With no wreckage to use as evidence, the Marine Board of Investigation stated, "…the exact cause of the loss of the *Marine Sulphur Queen* cannot be determined." However, the board concluded that either a massive explosion or bad weather may have caused a break in the ship's hull. Water would have poured in, likely breaking the ship in half and causing it to sink rapidly below the surface.

As for the men aboard? Some may have died as the ship sank. Others may have been alive in the water for a time. For those men, a few of the retrieved items hinted at their ultimate fate. The Coast Guard report stated, "Numerous tears on the life jackets indicated attack by predatory fish." There are many sharks in this area.

While some say the *Marine Sulphur Queen* and all aboard were victims of the mysterious Bermuda Triangle, others say the facts point to a tragedy at sea.

Left: Wreckage from the *Marine Sulphur Queen*, including part of the ship's name board, was collected and brought to the United States Coast Guard Headquarters. Tragically, neither the ship nor any of the crew were ever found.

WITCHCRAFT: THERE AND GONE

Dan Burack, a Miami, Florida, businessman, was an experienced sailor. His 23-foot (7-m) cabin cruiser, the *Witchcraft*, was equipped for safety. Not only was it stocked with life jackets, floatable seat cushions, and flares, it was also equipped with a flotation device in the hull that made the boat virtually unsinkable. If the *Witchcraft* filled with water, the hull would still remain afloat, giving its passengers something to hang on to until help arrived.

On Friday, December 22, 1967, Burack invited his friend, Father Patrick Horgan, to join him on a short cruise to see the Christmas lights of Miami. The local newspaper's small-boat forecast for that day: "Winds 10 to 20 knots, seas four to six feet, inland waters choppy."

When the two friends were about one mile (1.6 km) out from Miami Beach, the *Witchcraft* struck something in the water. Burack seemed calm when he sent an emergency radio transmission to the Coast Guard. He informed them that something was wrong with his boat and that he needed a tow back to Miami. Burack said that he was near buoy marker #7. He did not sound scared or frantic, nor did he say that his boat was sinking. With instructions from the Coast Guard to shoot off a flare in about 20 minutes, Burack signed off. He was never seen or heard from again.

Below: A cabin cruiser similar to Dan Burack's missing boat, the *Witchcraft*.

The Coast Guard rescue boat took off immediately, searching the area that Burack had given as his position. They watched for the expected signal flare, but it never came. More boats joined in the search, but the *Witchcraft* was never found.

What happened to this "unsinkable" cabin cruiser? What kept the two men from shooting a flare to alert their rescuers? Some say it was odd forces in the Bermuda Triangle. Others point to the fact that the winds and choppy seas may have flooded the powerless cabin cruiser. And at night, in rough seas, without an exact position for rescuers to search, the Atlantic Ocean is a whole lot of extreme blackness. Finding one small cabin cruiser can be next to impossible.

However, the fact that no wreckage or bodies were ever found has led many people to wonder what really happened to the mysterious *Witchcraft*.

Above: A sailboat in rough seas. The *Witchcraft* may have gone down at night in this type of dangerous water.
Left: A Coast Guard boat near a numbered buoy. On the night of December 22, 1967, Dan Burack reported that he was near buoy marker #7. However, neither he or the *Witchcraft* was ever found.

THE FOG: A SURVIVOR'S STORY

At 3:00 P.M. on December 4, 1970, pilot Bruce Gernon took off from Andros Island in the Bahamas in his Beechcraft Bonanza A36 airplane. He headed west for a quick trip to Florida. His father and one other passenger came along for the ride. Gernon hadn't been in the air long when he spied a large, eye-shaped cloud hovering in his path. All around were blue skies, and the current weather reports were good, so Gernon continued traveling toward the puffy cloud, expecting to fly quickly in and out of it. However, the cloud began growing, turning into an intense cumulus cloud that surrounded the plane.

By this time, Gernon's plane was near the Bimini Islands. The cloud produced bright white flashes. The flashes didn't act like normal lightning. Instead, they were intense, short bursts of light. Gernon tried to fly out of the cloud, but it seemed to grow around him. Still seeking an escape, Gernon finally noticed a U-shaped opening in the cloud. He quickly steered toward the opening. As he began flying through it, the U-shape fell in on itself, turning into an O-shaped tunnel.

Gernon sped through the cloud tunnel, increasing speed as he noticed the opening begin to shrink in towards the plane. As he finally roared out of the end of the tunnel, he glanced back and saw the cloud collapse onto itself.

Gernon wondered what he had just flown through, but he didn't have much time to think about it. Now the plane was encased in a gray, hazy fog. He couldn't see the sun, the ocean, or land. His instruments weren't working. Gernon was afraid he was flying through some kind of "electronic fog."

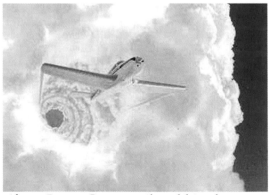

Above: Bruce Gernon piloted his plane through an O-shaped tunnel in the cloud.

Contacting the Miami air-traffic control tower, Gernon asked if they could spot him. After a few minutes, the controller radioed that they had found a plane over Miami Beach. Was that him? Gernon didn't think so. He should have been closer to the Bimini Islands.

But the radar signal was indeed his plane. Gernon discovered his error as the cloud began to break apart into ribbons, with blue sky shining through. Greatly relieved, Gernon flew on, now headed for Palm Beach, Florida, where he safely landed his plane.

But something odd had happened. It should have taken Gernon 75 minutes to travel from Andros Island to Palm Beach. He had done it in 47 minutes. What happened to the other 28 minutes? It could have been blamed on a faulty watch, but Gernon's father and their passenger's watches all indicated the same time.

Somehow, someway, Gernon lost nearly 30 minutes in the Bermuda Triangle. He wondered if the fog was some kind of time-travel tunnel. If he hadn't flown out of the fog when he did, would it have destroyed his plane? Gernon believes so. Thirty years later, Gernon put his ideas into a book entitled *The Fog*. While some scoff at the idea of time travel, others believe that Gernon may have survived what killed so many others. Perhaps this "electronic fog" is some type of natural occurrence, maybe even triggered by the metal of a plane or ship. Is this the phenomenon that causes compasses and other equipment to fail? Perhaps there is more to the legend of the Bermuda Triangle than we know.

Above: Bruce Gernon with his Beechcraft Bonanza A36 airplane in 1970.

Below: Gernon broke through the mysterious fog surrounding his plane, flying on to land safely.

EXPLAINING THE BERMUDA TRIANGLE

Explanations about the Bermuda Triangle's secrets have come from many sources. Researchers, scientists, historians, survivors, as well as friends and family members of those lost in its waters, have theories about the strange powers the area holds.

Below: An illustration of an alien ship over a coastal location. The Bermuda Triangle is an area with one of the most reports of UFO sightings.

Aliens

Some people believe that aliens may be in this area, and that these extraterrestrials have taken ships, planes, and crews to study. Reports of unidentified lights and mysterious objects have been documented for hundreds of years, but no scientific proof has been found. Most researchers believe the lights and objects occur naturally. Still, this area has one of the highest UFO sightings in the world. Can all these people be wrong?

Gulf Stream

The Gulf Stream is like a river in the Atlantic Ocean. This fast ocean current flows from the Gulf of Mexico toward Newfoundland, Canada. A ship caught in the Gulf Stream could easily be transported far from its original destination. Wreckage would also be quickly lost in the swift Gulf Stream.

Topography

Some of the deepest underwater drop-offs in the world are in the Bermuda Triangle. These great trenches are like giant black holes in the underwater landscape. Whatever goes in is never seen again. It is likely that the wreckage of a number of "missing" ships simply disappeared into one of these deep trenches.

Electronic Fog

Some believe that a combination of atmosphere, humidity, and the metal of planes or ships creates a kind of electromagnetic field, or fog, that seems to stick to the vessels. More than one commander has reported this odd phenomenon happening in the Bermuda Triangle. This theory is being studied by scientists.

Methane Gas

Rotting sea organisms create something called methane gas. Trapped inside the ocean floor, this gas has been found in the Bermuda Triangle area. If freed by a landslide or an underwater earthquake, a large bubble of gas erupts upward, causing the water to become much less dense. A vessel in the area would sink rapidly. Although no one has seen this happen to a ship, oil-drilling rigs have sunk because of escaping methane gas.

Above: A small plane flies into clouds. Several pilots have reported odd electromagnetic fields in the Bermuda Triangle.

Above: A waterspout is a tornado at sea.

Weather

Because of its location, the Bermuda Triangle creates its own weather patterns. It can go from clear to rough, and back to clear, in a short period of time. Sometimes remote storms do not even show up on weather-tracking devices. Waterspouts, which are tornados at sea, can easily destroy small ships and planes, leaving nothing to be found.

Earthquakes and Rogue Waves

The Bermuda Triangle is also prone to underwater earthquakes. This shifting of the ocean's floor may cause rogue waves. Also known as freak waves, these terrifying walls of water can reach heights as big as 100 feet (30 m). Many an unsuspecting ship has been blasted by these monster waves. Dr. Wolfgang Rosenthal, a German scientist studying rogue waves, states, "They are more frequent than

Above: A rogue wave about to break over a ship's bow.

we expected." These 8- to 10-story-tall waves have struck, damaged, and sometimes swamped merchant and cruise ships. There is little warning before a watery giant strikes. It is very possible that several of the Bermuda Triangle's victims were hit by one of these giant waves.

Heavy Traffic & Human Error

The Bermuda Triangle is one of the most traveled areas in the world, so it is no surprise that there are many accidents. Just as a busy city street will have more accidents than a quiet country road, this area is no different. Both the U.S. Coast Guard and Lloyd's of London, a company that insures large vessels and their loads, have stated that the risk factor in the Bermuda Triangle is the same as any other heavily trafficked ocean area. Despite this fact, people continue searching for answers to the unsolved mysteries of the Bermuda Triangle.

GLOSSARY

BUOY MARKER
In the United States, buoys are placed to help boaters navigate on the water. Buoys are designed, built, and maintained by the U.S. Coast Guard. Some buoys are lighted or have bells to help warn people of hazards in the water.

DITCH
An emergency or forced landing of a plane onto a body of water.

EXTRATERRESTRIAL
Something that comes from outside the earth or its atmosphere. An alien from another planet may also be referred to as an extraterrestrial.

FLOTATION DEVICE
Rescue equipment used to keep someone or something floating above water. Life jackets and life rings are examples of personal flotation devices. A boat may also have buoyant material installed in the hull (the main body of the ship) to keep the vessel floating even if it begins to sink.

GULF STREAM
An ocean current that begins in the Gulf of Mexico, travels northward along the United States coast up to Newfoundland, Canada, and then continues eastward as the North Atlantic Current. The Gulf Stream is warm, fast-moving, and relatively narrow, like a river within an ocean.

IFF
IFF stands for "Identification Friend or Foe." This emergency radar signal is used by the military to find and locate lost or downed planes.

NAVIGATOR
A person in charge of plotting the direction of ships, planes, or other forms of transportation. Historically, a navigator used the sun and stars to find their way. As time passed, maps and special instruments were used. Today, many people navigate using GPS, the Global Positioning System, which uses orbiting satellites to pinpoint a location.

PREDATORY FISH

Fish that eat other fish or animals. Sharks, barracudas, swordfish, marlin, and rays are examples of predatory fish.

RADAR

A way to find planes, ships and other objects. Radar stands for <u>ra</u>dio <u>d</u>etection <u>an</u>d <u>r</u>anging. The system sends out high-frequency electromagnetic waves, which bounce off any objects they hit, reflecting back to the source.

SIGNAL FLARE

A vividly glowing object that is shot into the sky to act as a signal for finding someone. Boats and planes often carry flare guns to shoot a fireworks-like signal high into the sky to signal for emergency help.

TOPOGRAPHY

A detailed physical description of a place or area. The topography of the underwater seafloor may include deep trenches, as well as tall rocky areas.

WATERSPOUT

A spinning column of air, water, and spray that forms over water. It is like a tornado.

Above: A waterspout is observed by air and sea vessels.

INDEX